1) Introduction: Investing in 2025

2) Understanding the 2025 Investment Environment

3) Fundamentals of Investing in 2025

4) Emerging Investment Trends

5) Strategic Investment Approaches

6) Risk Management and Investor Protection

7) Tools and Resources for Investors

8) Investing in a Digital Economy

9) Investing Beyond 2025: Future Prospect

Introduction: Investing in 2025

Purpose and scope

In the fast changing world of global finance and economics, the goal of this book is to provide a thorough guide to investing as we approach 2025. This guide is intended to not only inform, but also empower investors at all levels with the knowledge and vision required to handle the difficulties of the future years. By focusing on the strategic implications of current economic trends and forthcoming prospects, this book intends to provide readers with the tools they need to make informed investment decisions adapted to the realities of 2025 and beyond.

This book covers a study of the current economic and financial landscape, an exploration of significant trends influencing the future of investment, and practical tactics for capitalizing on these trends. It will discuss the necessity of forward-thinking investing strategies that take into account technological improvements, regulatory changes, and global economic upheavals. Examining these aspects will provide readers with a better understanding of how to position their portfolios for long-term growth and resilience in the years running up to 2025.

An Overview of the Current Economic and Financial Landscape.

To understand the framework in which investors will operate in 2025, consider the current economic and financial situation. As of 2024, global economies are dealing with a complex mix of problems and possibilities. Major economic indicators such as GDP growth rates, inflation levels, and employment data show various degrees of stability and uncertainty among areas.

Recent geopolitical developments have had a substantial impact on financial markets, influencing investor sentiment and volatility. The aftermath of these events has highlighted the interconnectivity of global economies and the need of geopolitical risk management in investing strategy.

In the meantime, technological innovations continue to change the financial industry. The rise of fintech innovations, blockchain technologies, and artificial intelligence (AI) is transforming traditional financial services, opening up new opportunities for investment and efficiency. These developments are more than just trends; they are fundamental shifts that investors must grasp and adapt to in order to profit on rising opportunities while mitigating risks.

Why Investment in 2025 is Critical

Investing in 2025 is crucial due to numerous key factors influencing the global economic landscape:

Economic and market forecasts indicate that by 2025, the global economy would have undergone substantial upheavals. Emerging markets are likely to play a critical role in global growth, opening up new investment opportunities in sectors such as technology, healthcare, and renewable energy. Understanding these forecasts enables investors to stay ahead of market trends and capitalize on new possibilities.

Technological Advancements: The high pace of technological innovation is expected to accelerate even further by 2025. Investments in AI, automation, and digital infrastructure will transform sectors and open up new economic opportunities. Companies that successfully integrate these technologies into their business models are likely to outperform their competitors, making them attractive investment opportunities for forward-thinking investors.

Environmental, Social, and Governance (ESG) Factors: Investors are increasingly valuing sustainability and ethical behaviors in their investment decisions. ESG considerations not only correspond with societal expectations, but they help reduce the risks connected with climate change and regulatory oversight. Investing in companies with strong ESG frameworks not only has a good environmental and social impact, but also improves long-term financial performance.

Long-term Financial Security: As global demographics shift and life expectancies rise, the significance of long-term financial planning grows. Investing in diversified portfolios that balance risk and return can provide financial security and stability, especially during difficult economic times. Planning for retirement and future financial goals necessitates the smart allocation of resources that account for market changes and economic cycles.

Understanding the 2025 Investment Environment.

Economic Trends and Forecasts for 2025

As investors look ahead to 2025, understanding the economic landscape is critical for making sound decisions. Economic trends and predictions offer a road map for identifying growth prospects and potential threats that may affect investing strategy.

Global Economic Outlook:

GDP Growth Rates: Projections show that growth rates will vary by location. Emerging markets, aided by demographic trends and technology improvements, are likely to outperform industrialized economies.

Inflation and Interest Rates: Central bank actions will be crucial in managing inflationary pressures and keeping interest rates stable. These factors influence borrowing costs and investment returns, which affect asset prices.

Sectorial Analysis:

Technology: Advancements in artificial intelligence, blockchain, and digital infrastructure will fuel industry-wide innovation. Investments in technology-driven enterprises stand to gain from disruptive technologies that shape consumer behavior and corporate operations.

Healthcare: As populations age and healthcare spending rises, medicines, biotechnology, and telemedicine are poised for growth. Investors can benefit from innovations that improve healthcare delivery and patient outcomes.

Renewable Energy: The transition to sustainable energy sources is a global priority, bolstered by legislative incentives and consumer demand. Investments in renewable energy projects and clean technologies support environmental aims while also providing possible benefits.

Regional insights:

Asia-Pacific: Rapid urbanization and digitization are propelling economic growth, with China and India leading the way in consumer markets and technological investments.

Europe: Economic recovery is aided by fiscal stimulus measures and green policies that promote opportunities in renewable energy, sustainable infrastructure, and digital transformation.

Americas: The US economy continues to innovate in the technology and healthcare areas, while Latin America offers potential in natural resources and developing markets.

Risk Factors:

Geopolitical Uncertainty: Trade tensions, political unrest, and regulatory changes can all affect global supply networks and investor confidence. Mitigating geopolitical risks with diversified portfolios and hedging methods is critical for protecting investment portfolios.

Global geopolitical influences on investments.

Geopolitical dynamics have a profound impact on investment landscapes by influencing regulatory regimes, market stability, and investor confidence. Understanding these effects is critical in predicting hazards and discovering opportunities in the run-up to 2025.

Trade Policy and Tariffs:
Ongoing trade conflicts between major economies, such as those between the United States and China, have an impact on market volatility and sector-specific hazards. Tariff regulations and retaliatory measures affect multinational firms' supply chains and profitability, necessitating flexible investment strategies.

Political Stability and Regulatory Change:
Political transitions and policy adjustments in key regions can be unpredictable for investment. Changes in regulatory frameworks, tax policies, and environmental standards all have an impact on corporate operations and profitability.

Engaging in geopolitical risk analysis and scenario planning allows for proactive risk management and strategic decision making.

Regional conflict and security risks:
Geopolitical disputes, regional instability, and security challenges all pose direct hazards to investment in afflicted areas. Geopolitical risk variables, such as military tensions and terrorism, influence asset allocation strategies and contingency plans.

Impact on emerging markets:
Emerging markets are vulnerable to geopolitical instability, which affects investor confidence and capital flows. Assessing political stability, governance quality, and rule of law enables educated investment decisions in emerging economies.

Technological Advancements Shape Investment Opportunities.

As the year 2025 approaches, technological innovation is altering sectors and opening up new investment opportunities. Understanding these breakthroughs is critical for identifying growth industries and tailoring investing strategies to take advantage of rising trends.

Artificial Intelligence:

AI technologies improve decision-making processes, automate operations, and increase efficiencies in industries such as banking, healthcare, and manufacturing.
Investments in AI-powered businesses and technology use predictive analytics, natural language processing, and machine learning algorithms to improve corporate processes and customer experiences.

Blockchain and digital assets:

Blockchain technology makes transactions more secure and transparent, transforming financial services, supply chain management, and digital identity verification. Investments in blockchain-based systems and cryptocurrencies present prospects for decentralized finance (DeFi), asset tokenization, and cross-border payment innovation.

Internet of things (IoT):

IoT connectivity provides real-time data collecting and analysis, which boosts production and operational efficiencies in areas including agriculture, logistics, and smart cities.

Investing in IoT infrastructure, sensor technology, and data analytics solutions promotes sustainable development and urban resilience.

Green Technology:

Innovations in renewable energy, energy storage, and sustainable infrastructure meet environmental concerns and regulatory needs.

Investments in green technology such as solar power, electric vehicles, and smart grid solutions help to achieve carbon neutrality while also creating long-term benefit for investors.

Cybersecurity:

Cyber dangers pose substantial risks to organizations and consumers in today's increasingly digital economy. Investing in cybersecurity technologies and risk management solutions safeguards sensitive information and improves digital resilience.

Fundamentals of Investing for 2025

Investing in 2025 necessitates a comprehensive grasp of core concepts that can endure market volatility, seize varied opportunities, and fit with changing societal expectations. This chapter examines basic principles of investing in a changing environment, emphasizes the importance of diversification and asset allocation, and dives into the growing influence of environmental, social, and governance (ESG) factors on investment decisions.

Key Principles of Investing in a Volatile Market

Navigating a dynamic market landscape necessitates commitment to core concepts that minimize risk while maximizing long-term gains.

Risk Management Strategies:

Asset Allocation: Managing risk and return by diversifying assets among asset classes (equities, bonds, cash equivalents, etc.) based on risk tolerance and investment goals.

Portfolio hedging is the use of derivative instruments (options, futures) to mitigate downside risk and reduce portfolio volatility during market downturns.

Stop-loss Orders: Using predetermined sell orders to limit losses and preserve capital in the face of adverse market moves.

Long-term investment horizon:

Buy and Hold Strategy: Investing in fundamentally sound firms or assets with growth potential and holding them for long periods of time to reap the benefits of compounding profits.

Value investing entails identifying inexpensive stocks based on intrinsic value criteria (price-to-earnings ratio, book value) and capitalizing on market inefficiencies to generate possible upside returns.

Behavioral finance considerations:
Emotional discipline is avoiding impulsive investing decisions motivated by fear or greed and sticking to a disciplined investment strategy that is linked with financial objectives.
Contrarian investing is the practice of capitalizing on market emotion extremes by purchasing oversold assets or selling overbought securities in order to profit from market inefficiencies.

Continuous monitoring and adjustments:
Portfolio rebalancing is periodically altering asset allocations to maintain goal risk levels while capitalizing on changing market circumstances.
Market research and due diligence entails thoroughly analyzing economic statistics, sector trends, and company fundamentals in order to make informed investment decisions.
The significance of diversification and asset allocation

Diversification and asset allocation are fundamental principles that reduce risk and improve portfolio performance under a variety of market scenarios.

Risk reduction and return maximization:
Asset diversification is the process of spreading investments across asset classes, industries, and geographical locations in order to reduce concentration risk and increase portfolio resilience.

Correlation Management: Choosing assets with low correlation coefficients to reduce portfolio volatility and maximize risk-adjusted returns.

Strategic asset allocation models:
Modern Portfolio Theory (MPT) is the use of mathematical models to create portfolios that achieve the best risk-reward balance based on an individual's risk tolerance and investment goals.
Dynamic Asset Allocation is the process of adjusting asset allocations in response to changing market conditions, economic cycles, and investment possibilities.

Sector and Geographical Exposure:

Sector Rotation: Moving investments between sectors to capitalize on emerging trends and sector-specific development possibilities while mitigating sector risks.
Global Diversification: Investing in worldwide markets to gain access to a variety of economic cycles, regulatory regimes, and growth opportunities that extend beyond home borders.

Portfolio Risk Management:

Tailored Risk Profiles: Aligning asset allocations with individual risk profiles, time horizons, and financial objectives to maximize risk-adjusted returns.
Stress testing and scenario analysis are used to measure portfolio resilience in severe market conditions and adjust asset allocation strategies accordingly.

The Influence of Environmental, Social, and Governance (ESG) Factors on Investment

ESG factors are becoming increasingly important in investment decision-making, reflecting broader cultural expectations and regulatory frameworks.

Environmental Factors:

Climate Change Risks: Evaluate carbon footprint, environmental sustainability practices, and exposure to climate-related risks (physical and regulatory) in investment portfolios.

Renewable Energy Investments: Investing in firms and initiatives that promote sustainable energy solutions and help the economy transition to a low-carbon future.

Social Factors:

Labor Practices and Human Rights: When evaluating investments, consider companies' social responsibility programs, workforce diversity, and adherence to fair labor standards.

Community impact refers to efforts that promote favorable social outcomes, such as affordable housing, healthcare access, and community development activities.

Governance Factors:
Corporate Governance Standards: Evaluate board diversity, CEO remuneration policies, and shareholder rights to guarantee strong governance and transparency.
Ethical Business Practices: Investing in companies with high ethical standards, anti-corruption measures, and accountability procedures to reduce governance risks.

Integration with Investment Strategies:
ESG Integration: Using ESG criteria in investment analysis and decision-making to improve risk management, long-term performance, and stakeholder value creation.
effect Investing is the practice of allocating capital to firms and funds that provide verifiable social and environmental effect in addition to financial returns, hence promoting sustainable development.

Emerging Investment Trends

Investors planning for 2025 must identify and capitalize on rising trends that promise growth, innovation, and sustainability. This chapter delves into the dynamic landscape of emerging countries, the boom in sustainable and impact investing, and the disruptive prospects offered by fintech and blockchain technology. Analysis of Emerging Markets and sectors.

Overview of emerging markets:

Regional Growth Dynamics: Examining the economic prospects and growth rates of key rising economies such as China, India, Brazil, and Southeast Asia.
Consumer Demographics: Understanding demographic trends, urbanization rates, and expanding middle-class spending patterns that influence demand across industries.

Sectoral Opportunities: Identifying promising sectors, such as technology, healthcare, consumer goods, and infrastructure, that will gain from population changes and economic transformation.

Investment Strategies for Emerging Markets: Risk vs. reward: Using political stability, regulatory frameworks, and currency risks to develop risk-adjusted investing strategies.

Sectoral Focus: Prioritizing areas that are poised for growth, innovation, and competitive advantage in emerging market economies.

Long-Term Outlook: Using long-term investing horizons to seize growth opportunities while navigating short-term market volatility.

Challenges and considerations:

Currency Volatility: Managing exposure to currency volatility and employing hedging measures to protect investment returns.

Governance and Transparency: Assessing corporate governance processes, regulatory compliance, and transparency standards to reduce investment risk.

Rise of Sustainable and Impact Investing

The Evolution of Sustainable Investment:

Environmental Considerations: Including environmental sustainability criteria in investment decisions to reduce climate change risks and increase resource efficiency.

Social impact refers to investments that promote positive social outcomes such as education, healthcare access, and community development.

Governance Standards: Investing in companies with strong governance systems and ethical business practices to increase shareholder value and reduce governance risks.

Impact Investing Strategy:

Measurable Impact: Investments are evaluated based on their ability to provide measurable social and environmental impact in addition to financial rewards.

Sectoral Focus: Allocating money to areas such as renewable energy, sustainable agriculture, affordable housing, and clean technology that help to achieve sustainable development goals.

Meeting growing investor demand for ethical investments that reflect personal values while also contributing to a more egalitarian and sustainable global economy.

Integration with Mainstream Investing:

ESG Integration: Adding environmental, social, and governance (ESG) elements to standard investing techniques to improve risk management and long-term performance.

Corporate involvement: Working with businesses to improve their ESG practices, transparency, and stakeholder involvement through active ownership and shareholder activism.

Regulatory Landscape: Responding to changing regulatory frameworks and disclosure requirements for sustainable finance and responsible investing.

Opportunities in Fintech and Blockchain Technology

FinTech Innovation Landscape:

Digital payments and banking are transforming financial services with digital payment systems, mobile banking apps, and peer-to-peer lending platforms.

Blockchain applications are expanding beyond cryptocurrencies to include smart contracts, decentralized finance (DeFi), and asset tokenization for increased security and efficiency.

Regulatory Evolution: Managing regulatory hurdles and compliance obligations while leveraging fintech technologies to improve operations and consumer experiences.

Investment Potential in Fintech:

Venture Capital and Startups: We invest in fintech startups and early-stage companies that use technology to disrupt traditional financial services and promote innovation.

Partnerships and Collaborations: Investigating potential strategic partnerships between fintech companies, financial institutions, and technology providers to expedite digital transformation and market expansion.

Consumer Adoption: We anticipate a shift in consumer behavior towards digital banking, online investing platforms, and personalized financial management tools.

Blockchain Technological Advancements: Decentralized Applications (dApps): Advancing the development of decentralized applications in industries such as supply chain management, healthcare, and real estate. Asset tokenization is the process of using blockchain-based systems to provide fractional ownership and trade of digital assets, real estate properties, and intellectual property rights.

Security and Transparency: Blockchain technology is being used to improve transaction security, data privacy, and auditability, hence increasing confidence and efficiency in global marketplaces.

Strategic Investment Approaches

Investing strategically in 2025 necessitates a deliberate approach that blends long-term growth goals with tactical modifications to capitalize on changing market opportunities. This chapter distinguishes between long-term and short-term investment strategies, investigates tactical allocation options pertinent to 2025, and provides case studies of effective investment strategies that demonstrate concepts and outcomes.

Long-term Versus Short-term Investment Strategies

Long-term Investment Strategy:
Goal-Oriented Investing: Matching investments to specified financial objectives and time frames, such as retirement planning, education funding, or wealth preservation.

Asset Accumulation: Creating diversified portfolios of shares, bonds, real estate, and other investments to generate long-term gain.

Compound Growth: Using the power of compounding returns by reinvesting dividends and capital gains to maximize wealth creation over time.

Risk Tolerance and Volatility Management: Using risk management tactics like dollar-cost averaging and periodic rebalancing to navigate market volatility and protect money.

Short-term Investment Strategy:

Market timing is taking advantage of short-term market inefficiencies and price volatility to make quick profits using active or swing trading tactics.

Sector Rotation: Investing in different sectors and asset classes based on economic data, sector performance, and market trends to maximize profits.

Opportunistic Investments: Taking advantage of immediate possibilities, such as initial public offerings

(IPOs), earnings announcements, or geopolitical developments, to profit from market changes.
Liquidity management entails maintaining enough liquidity to capitalize on market opportunities and meet short-term financial obligations without jeopardizing long-term investment goals.

Risk Considerations:
Risk vs. Reward Trade-offs: How to balance risk tolerance and return expectations when allocating cash between long-term investments and short-term trading activities.
Behavioral finance factors include recognizing psychological biases, such as overconfidence or loss aversion, that influence decision-making in short-term trading versus disciplined long-term investing.
Performance Evaluation: The monitoring and evaluation of long-term and short-term investment strategies against set benchmarks and targets in order to optimize portfolio outcomes.

Tactical Allocation Strategy for 2025

Dynamic asset allocation:
Strategic asset allocation entails creating portfolios with optimal allocations to asset classes such as equities, fixed income, commodities, and cash equivalents based on long-term risk-return goals. Tactical Asset Allocation entails dynamically adjusting asset allocations in response to changing market conditions, economic cycles, and sector-specific opportunities to improve portfolio performance.

Sector and Geographic Diversification:
Allocating capital across sectors and regions to capitalize on growth possibilities and reduce concentration risks in 2025's changing global market scenario.

Factor-Based Investment:
Smart Beta techniques: Using factor-based investing techniques including value, growth, momentum, and low volatility to boost risk-adjusted returns and meet specific investment goals.

Factor Rotation: Changing assets between factors based on market conditions and economic indicators in order to capitalize on factor premiums and reduce portfolio volatility.

Alternative Investment:

Private equity and venture capital are investments in private corporations, startups, and growth-stage enterprises that seek to produce alpha and diversify portfolio risk outside standard asset classes.

Real Assets:

Investing funds in tangible assets such as real estate, infrastructure, and commodities to protect against inflation, diversify portfolios, and capitalize on income-generating possibilities.

Hedge Funds and Absolute Return techniques:

Using alternative investment techniques such as long-short equities, global macro, and arbitrage to generate good returns regardless of market direction or traditional asset class performance.

Case Studies for Successful Investment Strategies

Technology Sector Growth:

Case Study 1: An analysis of an investment portfolio that profited from the exponential expansion of technological companies, such as cloud computing, artificial intelligence, and digital transformation projects.
Key success factors include strategic allocation to high-growth sectors, thorough due diligence on breakthrough technology companies, and aggressive portfolio rebalancing to capitalize on developing market trends.

ESG Integration and Sustainable Investment:

Case Study 2: An examination of a diverse portfolio that incorporated environmental, social, and governance (ESG) criteria into investment decisions, focusing on companies with good sustainability practices and ethical governance. Impact measurement is the evaluation of measurable social and environmental impacts in addition to financial returns, which highlights investor need for responsible investing and long-term value generation.

Global Macro Investment Strategy:

Case Study 3: An examination of a global macro hedge fund's investing strategy, which employs macroeconomic analysis, geopolitical insights, and currency strategies to mitigate market volatility and generate alpha.

Risk management entails implementing risk mitigation measures such as currency hedging and portfolio diversification across geographies and asset classes in order to protect capital and improve portfolio resilience.

Risk Management and Investor Protection

Identifying and mitigating investment risks. Risk management is a critical practice in investment management that identifies, assesses, and mitigates many sorts of risks that could harm investment portfolios. Effective risk management methods are critical for protecting investors' wealth and meeting their financial objectives.

Here are specific insights on main risk kinds and mitigation strategies:

Market Risk:

Definition: Market risk is the potential for losses caused by fluctuations in market prices, such as equities prices, interest rates, and commodity prices.

Mitigation Strategy: Diversification across asset classes and geographic regions helps to mitigate risk. Hedging tactics, such as options and futures contracts, can help to reduce certain market exposures. Asset allocation based on risk tolerance and investment horizon is also an important factor in managing market risk.

Credit Risk:

Definition: Credit risk is the probability that a borrower or counterparty will fail to pay their financial obligations.

Mitigation Strategy: Before getting into financial transactions with counterparties, conduct a thorough credit investigation and due diligence. Collateral requirements and credit enhancement techniques, such as letters of credit or guarantees, can reduce credit risk exposure. Monitoring credit ratings and credit spreads allows for a continual evaluation of credit risk.

Liquidity Risk:

Definition: Liquidity risk is the danger of being unable to buy or sell investments quickly and at a reasonable price. **Mitigation Strategy:** Maintaining appropriate liquidity in investment portfolios to satisfy prospective cash flow requirements. Monitoring market liquidity and diversifying assets into liquid asset types. Stress-testing liquidity requirements in various market conditions to assure preparation.

Operational Risk:

Definition: Operational risk is caused by inadequate or failing internal procedures, systems, or human error.

Mitigation Strategy: Implementing strong internal controls, rules, and processes to reduce operational risks. Conducting routine audits and evaluations of operational processes to discover flaws and enhance controls. To reduce human error, staff should be trained on risk awareness and operating process compliance.

Regulatory Risk:

Definition: Regulatory risk is caused by changes in laws and regulations that may have an influence on investment strategies or impose compliance expenses.

Mitigation Strategy: Keeping up with regulatory developments through interactions with regulatory bodies, industry associations, and legal consultants. Adapting investing methods and structures to meet new requirements. Before entering new markets or asset classes, conduct regulatory due diligence to determine compliance risks.

The importance of due diligence and research.
Due diligence and research are critical to making sound investing decisions and protecting investors' interests.

Comprehensive due diligence and research processes include a detailed review of the financial, operational, and regulatory elements of potential investments.

Financial analysis:

Financial documents, such as income statements, balance sheets, and cash flow statements, are examined to determine profitability, liquidity, and solvency.

Using financial parameters such as return on investment (ROI), debt-to-equity ratio, and earnings per share (EPS) to assess financial health and performance.

Qualitative research:

Conducting industry analysis to better understand market dynamics, the competitive landscape, and development opportunities.

Assessing management quality and corporate governance standards to determine leadership competency and alignment with shareholder interests.

Risk Assessment:

Identifying and assessing risks related to the industry, market, and geopolitical environment.

Conducting scenario analysis and stress testing to measure investment resiliency under various economic scenarios.

Legal and Regulatory Compliance:

Ensure that investments conform with applicable rules, regulations, and tax requirements.

Examining legal documents, such as contracts and agreements, for any legal risks and responsibilities.

Long-term Performance:

Analyzing past performance and projecting future performance using economic forecasts and industry patterns.

Long-term investment viability is evaluated by assessing sustainability aspects such as environmental, social, and governance (ESG) standards.

Regulatory Changes affecting Investors in 2025

Regulatory changes have a substantial impact on the investing landscape, altering investment strategies, risk management techniques, and compliance obligations for investors.

Securities Regulations:

Changes to securities regulations controlling the issuing, trading, and reporting of stocks, bonds, and derivatives. Implementation of new regulations to improve market transparency and investor protection.

Tax Regulations:

Tax policy updates that affect investment returns, deductions, and reporting duties for investors.
Changes in capital gains tax rates, dividend tax treatment, and tax breaks for certain investments.

Consumer Protection Laws:

Increased consumer protections and disclosure requirements for financial products and services. Regulations are being implemented to prevent fraud, mis-selling, and unfair practices in the investing markets.

Environmental, Social, and Governance Regulations:

Integration of ESG elements into regulatory frameworks that influence investment decisions and disclosures. Companies are required to disclose ESG risks and initiatives, which influence investor preferences and corporate governance procedures.

Global Regulatory Harmonization:

Efforts to standardize regulatory standards between jurisdictions in order to promote cross-border investment and eliminate regulatory arbitrage.
Regulatory bodies work together to manage systemic risks and ensure financial stability in global markets.

Technology and Fintech Regulations:
Regulation of digital assets, blockchain technology, and fintech advances influence investment potential and hazards.

Adoption of regulatory frameworks to foster innovation while protecting investors from technological and cybersecurity risks.

Tools and Resources for Investors

Overview of Investment Platforms and Apps

Investment platforms and apps have revolutionized how individuals manage and execute their investment strategies. These digital tools provide accessibility, convenience, and a wide range of functionalities tailored to both novice and experienced investors.

Types of Investment Platforms

Investment platforms vary in scope and features, catering to different investor preferences and objectives:

- **Brokerage Platforms**: Offer trading services for stocks, bonds, options, and ETFs. Examples include Robinhood, E*TRADE, and TD Ameritrade.

- **Robo-Advisors**: Automated investment platforms that provide portfolio management based on algorithms and investor risk profiles. Examples include Betterment, Wealthfront, and Ellevest.

- **Crowdfunding Platforms**: Facilitate investment in startups, real estate projects, and peer-to-peer lending. Examples include Kickstarter, SeedInvest, and RealtyMogul.

- **Social Trading Platforms**: Enable investors to follow and replicate the trades of experienced traders. Examples include eToro, ZuluTrade, and Covestor.

Features and Benefits

Investment platforms and apps offer a variety of features that enhance investment management:

- **Real-time Market Data**: Access to live market prices, charts, and news updates.

- **Portfolio Tracking**: Monitor investment performance, asset allocation, and historical returns.

- **Research and Analysis Tools**: Fundamental and technical analysis tools to assess investment opportunities.

- **Educational Resources**: Tutorials, articles, and webinars to educate investors on financial markets and strategies.

- **Mobile Accessibility**: Ability to manage investments on-the-go via smartphones and tablets.

Considerations for Choosing an Investment Platform

When selecting an investment platform, investors should consider the following factors:

- **Fees and Commissions**: Compare trading fees, account maintenance fees, and additional costs for services.

- **Investment Options**: Availability of stocks, bonds, mutual funds, ETFs, and alternative investments.

- **User Interface**: Intuitive design and ease of navigation.

- **Security Features**: Encryption, two-factor authentication, and regulatory compliance.

- **Customer Support**: Access to responsive customer service and educational support.

Utilizing Data Analytics and AI in Investment Decisions

Data analytics and artificial intelligence (AI) are increasingly shaping investment strategies by providing sophisticated tools for data processing, pattern recognition, and predictive modeling.

Applications of Data Analytics and AI

- **Risk Management**: Utilize historical data and predictive analytics to assess and mitigate investment risks.

- **Portfolio Optimization**: Identify optimal asset allocation strategies based on historical performance and market trends.

- **Market Sentiment Analysis**: Analyze social media, news sentiment, and macroeconomic indicators to gauge market sentiment.

- **Algorithmic Trading**: Implement automated trading strategies based on predefined rules and algorithms.

- **Fraud Detection**: Identify irregularities and anomalies in financial transactions and trading activities.

Benefits of Data-driven Decision Making

- **Improved Accuracy**: Enhanced ability to analyze large datasets and identify meaningful patterns.
- **Efficiency**: Automation of routine tasks such as data processing and report generation.
- **Scalability**: Capability to handle large volumes of data and adapt to changing market conditions.
- **Competitive Advantage**: Gain insights and make informed decisions faster than traditional methods.

Challenges and Considerations

- **Data Quality**: Ensure data accuracy, completeness, and reliability for meaningful analysis.

- **Algorithm Transparency**: Understand the logic and assumptions underlying AI models to avoid unintended biases.

- **Regulatory Compliance**: Adhere to data privacy regulations and ethical standards in AI usage.

Importance of Financial Education and Continuous Learning

Financial education is essential for investors to develop the knowledge, skills, and confidence needed to make informed financial decisions and achieve long-term financial goals.

Foundations of Financial Education

- **Basic Financial Literacy**: Understanding concepts such as budgeting, saving, debt management, and compound interest.

- **Investment Principles**: Learning about asset classes, risk-return tradeoffs, diversification, and investment strategies.

- **Economic Fundamentals**: Understanding macroeconomic factors influencing financial markets and investment outcomes.

- **Legal and Regulatory Knowledge**: Awareness of investment regulations, tax implications, and investor protections.

Benefits of Continuous Learning

- **Adaptability**: Keep pace with evolving market trends, technologies, and regulatory changes.

- **Risk Management**: Develop skills to identify and mitigate investment risks effectively.

- **Enhanced Decision Making**: Make informed decisions based on updated knowledge and insights.

- **Empowerment**: Take control of personal finances and investment portfolios with confidence.

Resources for Financial Education

- **Online Courses and Webinars**: Platforms like Coursera, edX, and Khan Academy offer free and paid courses on finance and investing.

- **Books and Publications**: Reading books by renowned authors and financial experts to deepen knowledge.

- **Seminars and Workshops**: Attend industry conferences, workshops, and seminars to learn from professionals.

- **Financial Advisors**: Consult with certified financial planners (CFPs) or investment advisors for personalized guidance.

Investing in a Digital Economy

Investing in the digital economy encompasses a broad range of opportunities and sectors that are transforming industries and reshaping global markets. From e-commerce and digital currencies to cybersecurity and AI, investors can capitalize on these trends to achieve growth and diversification in their portfolios.

Opportunities in E-commerce, Digital Currencies, and Online Platforms

E-commerce:

The rise of e-commerce has revolutionized retail and consumer behavior, offering significant investment opportunities:

- **Market Growth**: Rapid expansion of online retail sales globally, driven by convenience and accessibility.
- **Platforms**: Investing in e-commerce platforms like Amazon, Alibaba, and Shopify that facilitate online transactions and digital storefronts.

- **Logistics and Infrastructure**: Investments in logistics companies and infrastructure supporting e-commerce supply chains.

Digital Currencies:

Digital currencies, including cryptocurrencies and stablecoins, have gained popularity as alternative forms of payment and investment:

- **Bitcoin and Ethereum**: Leading cryptocurrencies attracting investor interest due to their potential as stores of value and transactional mediums.
- **Blockchain Technology**: Investing in blockchain infrastructure and applications transforming finance, supply chains, and decentralized finance (DeFi).
- **Regulatory Landscape**: Considerations of regulatory developments impacting the adoption and valuation of digital currencies.

Online Platforms:

Investing in digital platforms beyond e-commerce that connect users, content, and services globally:

- **Social Media**: Platforms like Facebook (Meta), Twitter, and TikTok offering advertising revenue and user engagement opportunities.
- **Streaming Services**: Investments in streaming platforms like Netflix, Disney+, and Spotify that dominate digital content consumption.
- **Gig Economy**: Funding platforms facilitating gig work and freelancing, such as Uber, Upwork, and Fiverr.

Investing in Cybersecurity and Data Privacy Sectors

The increasing digitization of businesses and personal data has elevated the importance of cybersecurity and data privacy investments:

- **Cybersecurity Solutions**: Investing in companies providing cybersecurity software, threat detection, and incident response services.
- **Data Privacy Compliance**: Funding firms specializing in data protection, compliance with regulations like GDPR and CCPA.
- **Cyber Insurance**: Opportunities in the insurance sector offering coverage against cyber threats and data breaches.

Impact of AI and Automation on Investment Strategies

Artificial intelligence (AI) and automation are transforming industries by enhancing efficiency, decision-making, and operational capabilities:

- **Algorithmic Trading**: Investment in AI-powered trading algorithms analyzing market trends and executing trades automatically.
- **Predictive Analytics**: Utilizing AI to forecast market movements, customer behavior, and economic trends.

- **Automation in Industries**: Investments in companies adopting automation technologies to streamline operations and reduce costs.

- **Sectoral Impacts**: How AI and automation are reshaping industries like healthcare, manufacturing, and finance through robotics and machine learning.

Investing Beyond 2025: Future Prospect

Investing in the next decade is expected to see major changes motivated by global trends, economic changes, and technological developments. Understanding the forecasts, problems, possibilities, and tactics for adjusting to future changes becomes essential for investors trying to negotiate and seize developing chances as we look ahead beyond 2025.

Forecasts for the Decade Ahead in Investing

AI & Machine Learning: Growing application of AI-powered algorithms for trading, portfolio management, and risk assessment.

Blockchain and Digital Assets: Development of smart contracts, digital identification, and supply chain management among other blockchain uses outside cryptocurrencies.

Integration of IoT devices and data analytics for operational efficiency in sectors and predictive maintenance helps to create Internet of Things (IoT).

Mainstream acceptance of Environmental, Social, and Governance (ESG) principles in investment decision-making marks sustainable investing.

Growing investments aiming at quantifiable social and environmental effects alongside financial gains is known as impact investing.

Strengthening of rules supporting sustainable practices and disclosure obligations under influence of regulation.

Preferences for digital platforms, ESG-aligned investments, and financial product openness define millennial and Gen Z investors.

Investing possibilities in healthcare, elder living, and technologies suited for aging populations comes under the silver economy.

Geopolitical and Economic Trends:

Impact of trade policy, geopolitics tensions, and regional economic integration on investment flows globalizing against protectionism.

Emerging Markets: Urbanization, technology use, and middle-class consumption rising drive prospects for growth in these nations.

Difficulties and Prospectives for Worldwide Investors
One faces challenges as follows:

Geopolitical uncertainty, technological upheavals, and macroeconomic events have driven higher market volatility.

Navigating many regulatory environments across countries influencing investment strategies and compliance costs requires a degree of complexity. Rising dangers of cyberattacks on financial institutions call for strong security protocols.
Investing in disruptive technologies such artificial intelligence, biotechnology, renewable energy, and quantum computers will present opportunities.

Healthcare and Biotech: Possibilities in biopharmaceuticals, individualized treatment, and healthcare innovation.

Investments in smart cities, renewable energy, transportation, and environmentally friendly infrastructure projects—including smart buildings—should help to shape our future.

Digital Transformation: Development in e-commerce, digital payments, and online services influencing customer preferences and business models shapes behavior.

Investing in wellness, fitness, and sustainable food production that reflects evolving consumer lifestyles helps one.

Education and Upskill: Possibilities in online learning environments and workforce development to satisfy changing skill needs.

Approaches for Adjusting to Technological and Economic Changes Ahead:

Global diversification—that is, spreading investments throughout locations, asset classes, and sectors—allows one to control risk and seize development possibilities.

Allocation to alternative assets for diversity and better returns include real estate, venture capital, and private equity.

Conducting scenario analysis helps one to evaluate possible effects of geopolitical events, economic changes, and technology disturbances on risk management and resilience.

Stress testing helps to assess portfolio resilience under several market environments and stress scenarios.

Using artificial intelligence and data analytics for predictive analytics, risk management, and financial decision-making helps one embrace technology.

Blockchain and Digital Assets: Investigating prospects in digital currencies, tokenizing of assets, and distributed finance (DeFi).

Including ESG factors into investment plans will help to match investor preferences and legal obligations.

Allocating funds and projects with quantifiable social and environmental effects with financial rewards is the essence of impact investing.

Investing in continuous education and research will help one remain updated on industry trends, technology developments, and legislative changes.

Engaging industry professionals, going to conferences, and joining professional networks to share ideas and best practices helps one to network and cooperate.

In summary,

Beyond 2025, investing presents opportunities defined by technological innovation, demographic changes, and global economic trends as well as problems.

Anticipating and adjusting to these developments will help investors to control risks and position themselves to seize new chances. Navigating the changing terrain of global investing in the next decade will depend mostly on embracing technology, including ESG issues, diversifying portfolios, and keeping resilience through ongoing learning and strategic adaptation.

Non-Financial Advisor Non-Liability Statement Disclaimer:

The information provided in this publication is for educational and informational purposes only. It is not intended as financial or investment advice, nor is it a substitute for professional advice from a qualified financial advisor or investment manager.

Investing in cryptocurrencies or any other financial asset involves risk, and the reader should conduct their own research and seek the advice of a professional before making any investment decisions. The author does not assume any responsibility or liability for any losses or damages resulting from the use of the information provided.

Cryptocurrency markets are highly volatile and can experience significant fluctuations within short periods. Past performance is not indicative of future results. The reader should be aware of the risks involved, including the potential for loss of capital.

The views and opinions expressed in this publication are those of the author and do not necessarily reflect the official policy or position of any other agency, organization, employer, or company.

By accessing and using this information, the reader acknowledges and agrees that they bear full responsibility for their own investment decisions and actions. They also agree that the author is not responsible for any outcome or consequence of such decisions.

This disclaimer applies to all content within this publication, including text, images, links, and any other material presented.

www.ingramcontent.com/pod-product-compliance
Lightning Source LLC
Chambersburg PA
CBHW071959210526
45479CB00003B/1004